QUIET
DESTINY

ALOYSIUS K. ITOKA

Order this book online at **www.trafford.com**
or email orders@trafford.com

Most Trafford titles are also available at major online book retailers.

Printed in the United States of America.

ISBN: 978-1-4669-1257-1 (sc)
ISBN: 978-1-4669-1258-8 (e)

Library of Congress Control Number: 2012901380

Trafford rev. 03/14/2012

 www.trafford.com

North America & International
toll-free: 1 888 232 4444 (USA & Canada)
phone: 250 383 6864 ♦ fax: 812 355 4082

Table of Contents

DEDICATION

This book of poems is lovingly dedicated to the memory of my parents for their care and sacrifices made in my behalf during their lifetime.

To my parents and relatives whose unabated advice and examples encouraged me to be able to attain this goal.

To all those who in anyway assisted in its production particularly my nephew Francis M. Freeman who financially supported it, this work is humbly and sincerely dedicated.

INTRODUCTION

QUIET DESTINY, is a collection of poems, written by the author, for the entertainment of individuals at every level of experience; students and indeed anybody with an interest in poetry. These ideas which are in some cases imaginative, are also sometimes interwoven with realities; THE GOOD OLD DAYS; I HEARD NO ROOSTER CROW and LIVE NOT IN DISGRACE. For those who have poetic talents, these poems would be found most suitable for the styles are simple and can be easily understood. As you read through the lines you will observe that most of the poems have a high point of interest, and to achieve the intended pleasure each high point of interest musts be identified. They may appear a few strange words to the causal reader but the simplicity of the verses would in no way create the need for references.

The basic objective of these poems, however, is to motivate the talented, especially those of the younger generation who, for some reasons or excuses have not released these gifts which are often sometimes latent and bound to erupt at one time or another.

ABOUT THE AUTHOR

Mr. Aloysius K. Itoka was born of Mr. and Mrs. Joseph Itoka in Harper, Cape Palmas, Maryland County on July 27, 1929. He began his early studies at St. Mary's Catholic Elementary School in Nyaake Webbo where his parents were relocated. He then completed the St. Francis' School in Pleebo, Maryland County as a boarding student and completed the eighth grade in 1945. He continued his education at the St. Patrick's High School in Monrovia and obtained a Diploma in 1949. He enrolled at the Liberia College in 1950 and graduated in 1953 with a Bachelor of Arts Degree in Biology. Mr. Itoka worked for a short time with the National Public Health Service in Monrovia as a Clerk Typist assigned to the Deputy Director General of the Service, Dr. J. B. Titus, before returning to Harper, Maryland County as an Instructor of Biology in the Cape Palmas High School from 1955 to 1958. In 1959, he returned to Monrovia and entered the Foreign Service Institute and upon completion of the prescribed courses was assigned to the Embassy of Liberia in Bonn, Federal Republic of Germany and later to the Embassy of Liberia in Lagos, Nigeria. He returned to Monrovia and joined the staff of the William V.S Tubman College of Technology in Harper Maryland county in 1980 and remained until the civil war engulfed the country. He left Liberia in 2002 and sought refuge in the United States of America.

BRIEF INFORMATION
ABOUT THE BOOK

This book consists of poems depicting the senseless civil war that erupted in Liberia in 1989. The destruction of the country and complete breakdown of law and order accompanied by the killing of more than two hundred and fifty thousand people, while many fled the country for foreign parts, motivated the writing of these poems. As one of those who experienced the harsh and inhumane living conditions within the refugee camps, in neighboring La Cote d'Ivoire, where Liberians were most often manhandled, publicly humiliated and freely harassed and insulted, it is inconceivable why some of our own people, under the disguise of Freedom Fighters, could have meted out such pains and horrendous crimes against their fellow countrymen in the first place.

Liberia, as the first Independent Republic in Africa, had maintained a stable and peaceful nation over a hundred and fifty years, thus achieving a world-wide status and recognition among the comity of nations. The civil war however, with the cruel attempt of the so-called Freedom Fighters to eliminate the educated class, destruction of major infrastructures, uprooting facilities, destroying roads and bridges and the entire Civil Service of the country had thrown the country a hundred years backwards. Unless Liberians accept realities and are willing to work harder to harness whatever scarce resources now remain, eschew corruption, bribery and nepotism, the country's future will remain bleak and a squalid land be handed down to all generations and the country a disappointment to the African Continent.

THE GOOD OLD DAYS

Serene I sit on ends and wait;
No food or drink a sad situation;
A life of woe a dismal fate;
Some ray of hope my sole salvation.

They watched unmoved as we succumbed;
To days of grief and dreadful nights;
Hearts torn apart as unroofed homes;
Sadly yawning to claim our sights.

The nights were damp so cold and chill,
Rainstorms and winds are blowing wild;
Frail sighs of pain the tents stood still;
Homes split in twain a new born child.

Gone are the days when all was right,
Conceit, deceit now guide our ways;
Revengeful death disgusting blight,
Bring back once more the Good Old Days.

ALOYSIUS K. ITOKA

THE CAVALLA RIVER

Embankments high with hanging boughs,
Red, muddy Duo* white flowing suds;
Kiss headless corpse as a man plows,
Along sand=bars of birds and buds.

In small canoes they calmly sit,
Braving the crossings of the deep;
A day of gloom a monstrous pit;
Our breath withheld sometimes to weep.

"Let's go" it was so loud and clear,
The paddle dipped away they went;
"stop that", "sit down" good gracious dear,
Look at that leak we'll not relent

In haste they scuttle up the slopes,
Collecting Oil and Beans and Fish;
Few cups of rice and salt the hopes,
Of those who dared just for a dish.

The search for basic daily needs,
Remains unchanged each day the scene;
Oh save them from those fatal deeds,
And smooth their paths in ways unseen.

*DUO refers to the Cavalla River.

ALOYSIUS K. ITOKA

HAVE NO CONFIDENCE IN MAN

O faithful land of righteous men'
Where God's command supremely reigns;
Gold and Silver hopes of heathen
Are worthless things in HIS DOMAIN.

Many have become indeed rebellious,
Some friends of thieves we have been told;
The Name of God sounds melodious,
O lead us back into Your Fold.

We hail Leaders and advisors,
Such as we had in times long past;
Shield us from all vile pretenders,
By Thee O Lord our Lot is cast.

When pride has long been committed,
And Earthly arrogance debased;
You Alone will be Exalted,
As confidence in man erased.

ALOYSIUS K. ITOKA

HE IS LORD

Tell me not in simple phrases,
Horrors that I have long beheld;
Thousands groan in putrid marshes,
Towards which they were all misled.

Days that were so long and dreary,
Brought us evil and great sorrow;
Some maimed lay dying they being weary
Wait the lame for sad tomorrow.

So many precious lives were lost,
For lack of common faith and will;
Sinners rejoice at righteous cost;
Seek not revenge HE ruleth still.

He is Alive the GOOD BOOK says,
Trust not yourself have faith in God;
He is the Truth, the Light and the Way,
Be not afraid, HE IS THE LORD.

ALOYSIUS K. ITOKA

I HEARD NO ROOSTER CROW

The sun rose early on the morn,
Our shadows trailing on the sand;
Unending sounds of guns in turn,
Booming aloud throughout the land.

It's sad to say but true indeed,
I heard no Rooster Crow.

Throughout captured land we travelled,
Where many a fighter were deployed;
O'er death's dark vales we marveled,
At countless skulls that were destroyed,

It's sad to say but true indeed,
I heard no Rooster Crow

Along the road of blood and death,
Remorse of conscience filled to heart;
What had become of Mother Earth,
As sin of Cain will n'er depart,

ALOYSIUS K. ITOKA

It's sad to say but true indeed,
I heard no Rooster Crow

On sides of the old Plantation,
Among crops green 'neath rubber trees;
Decayed frames of God's creation,
Emitting stench with morning breeze,

It's sad to say but true indeed,
I heard no Rooster Crow

So bleak were the burnt out houses,
As caved in roofs under sunny skies;
Revealed skills lost for all ages;
By vain ambition in disguise,

It's sad to say but true indeed,
I heard no Rooster Crow

To bed that night I had reclined,
With fear and grim resignation;
All call for peace had been declined,
By vile and mean ostentation.,

I woke at dawn and true indeed,
I heard no Rooster Crow.

ALOYSIUS K. ITOKA

THE DISAPPOINTED POLICEMEN

To wish you luck I take my leave,
Intent to tread no more this road;
Since there are none that I believe,
From me do shear this awful load.

He took the wheels and swiftly sped,
Leaving a trailing smoke behind;
It rammed in head-long pedestrians fled,
Over looted goods of every kind.

The panicked clod lost his control,
As lives now rest in Hands of Time;
The car collided spewing petrol,
In scarlet dust of blood and slime.

The scene unleashed an angry crowd,
Who uttered several bitter words;
A frightened culprit no longer proud,
Now sat bemused against such odds.

ALOYSIUS K. ITOKA

Two cops appeared in dew so dense,
"Your license please" one calmly said;
In vain he searched with great pretense,
Neither at home was he prepared.

Then to the Chief at once they went,
With much excuses so often heard;
He pled in tears as he was sent,
To a crammed cell without his beard.

When late the cops returned that day,
The Chief had lunched with shrimp cocktail;
All cells were searched to their dismay;
Realized the culprit was on bail.

A fixed date was set for the trial,
Arranged so it be not deferred;
The chief who was not so congenial,
Had both the cops involved transferred.

The case was called up as assigned,
Both transferred cops were right on time;
Alert at what had been designed,
The Chief, they knew was not sublime.

The culprit took the stand at last,
And pleaded guilty as was charged;
The Judge refreshed from a repast,
Quickly had the man discharged.

The Chief was now a happy man,
When with smiles and joy he was told;
That the Judge who was of his Clan,
Had thrown the case out in the cold.

ALOYSIUS K. ITOKA

LIVE NOT IN DISGRACE

She left me on a rainy day in June,
Arrayed in plain neat dress of azure blue;
Her neck bedecked with gold of great fortune,
To me she said, "I'll soon come back to you".

Over the dress her long hair loosely hung,
Short quick steps gave life to a charming gait;
Low blowing wind her coat openly flung,
Revealing legs which led her through the narrow gate.

For fear that she might miss the only flight,
In haste that day to Robertsfield we drove;
My heart grew faint I realized not my plight,
When to the desert bird I sadly strove.

It was a light steel-plated plane of old,
Awaiting on the drenched and slippery runway;
As engine roared tear drops I could not hold,
Blurred stratus clouds that took my love away.

ALOYSIUS K. ITOKA

Come back to me O precious jewel of my eyes,
The vows you made indeed seem all in vain;
Your tender touch now thrust into the skies,
Is just a dream held captive in that plane.

So many years have now gone by my only love,
Those words of hope reflect your loving face;
If games you played were treasures from above,
Farewell, goodbye, I'll live not in disgrace.

LIZARDS, LIZARDS EVERYWHERE

I have never seen so many lizards,
Creeping about casually like drunkards;
They crawl and roam all over the place,
And some so bold to stare you in the face.
Even so bold they wink and stare,
Lizards, Lizards everywhere.

From Custom House where passengers embark,
To long huge buses resembling Noah's Ark;
Give them an inch, they sneak into your suit,
As agents from a reptile Institute.
That institute must be in a mess, I swear,
Lizards, Lizards everywhere.

At the bus stops you find these creatures,
Clutching and cringing on anything that features;
Leaders of tomorrow each armed with a rubber gun,
Carry strings of lizards dangling in the sun;
Those strings are no doubt someone's fare,
Lizards, lizards everywhere.

ALOYSIUS K. ITOKA

Along the busy road to Yamousoukro,
To the coastal city of San Pedro;
They always seem to be timing,
Road transport buses endlessly coming;
Coming with passengers as if from a fair,
Lizards, lizards everywhere.

One night I went to the roast meat stall,
And indeed did have a great ball;
The roast was fresh and tasted sweet,
With some brown powder sprinkled over the meat;
Juicy meat extra super rare,
Lizards, lizards everywhere.

Red head, tailless, short and long,
You often see them creeping along;
Just toss a crumb they know their tricks,
Most often even after six;
Though after six they do not care,
Lizards, lizards everywhere.

Back to camp I went at last,
And met inmates who were as usual on fast;
So as not to upset many a feeling,
I said nothing about the side eating;
That eating turned out to be a nightmare,
Lizards, lizards everywhere.

Next day in tents many who looked hungry,
Wanted to know why I was so merry;
I told them French bread was really a treat,
With brown powdered seasoning sprinkled over roasted
meat,
That roast meat would lead me to declare,
Lizards, lizards everywhere.

ALOYSIUS K. ITOKA

And so despondent feelings I could not uphold,
When with great amazement it was unfold;
That the brown dust which tasted so sweet,
Was ground, dried lizards sprinkled over the meat;
For love of roasted meat I became a square,
Lizards, lizards everywhere.

Too late now to find a solution,
But I have made another resolution;
To acquaint roasted meat eaters about that dust,
Brown dust which often helps to knock off the rust;
Rust here, or dust there,
Lizards lizards everywhere.

ALOYSIUS K. ITOKA

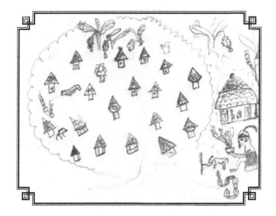

THE JUJUMAN

When evening breeze her crusted fetters break,
And sends red dust above the village streets;
The tides swell high above the village lake,
Flowing into the winding narrow creeks.

The vengeance spread along the mountain side,
Creating fear and havoc at her will;
Uprooting crops while deer and gazelles stride,
Over young growth and stumps without their fill.

Monkeys and Chimps were all in disarray,
Springing and swinging as the stubborn wind;
Violently slaying gibbons in its way,
Spared not a single kith or kin.

Unmindful of the damage that was done,
It swept across the slopes and rocky hills;
Destroying wide forest reserve begun,
Leaving behind ruins of worn out saw mills.

ALOYSIUS K. ITOKA

Her wrath continued through the gloomy night,
Sending tremors and chills in everyone;
They dare not sleep in spite of windows tight,
But stared with dread at what the wind had done.

The sun rose early at the break of day,
With villagers gossiping without fear;
Accepting roofs that had been blown away,
As Omen of a cursed forsaken year.

So to the Jujuman they quickly went,
Drums beat assembled men from far and wide;
A lady who had been his discontent,
Was the sole victim he must now deride.

A wife had been unfaithful to her vows,
That has brought misfortune to our town;
She must confess and pay a cost in cows,
"To please the GODS" he said, as he sat down.

The exploits of accused he knew too well,
So the snare prepared she could not escape;
She confessed and before her husband fell,
Naming a man strongly built like an Ape.

The Lover Boy to the charge consented,
Because he was known as a man of wealth;
And by rejecting what was requested,
Was, he knew, self confirmation of death.

The day for the sacrifice having been appointed,
Three cows five bags of rice imposed were paid;
The Jujuman performed as he was expected,
Displaying colorful charms and gambles on parade.

ALOYSIUS K. ITOKA

The Oracles having been consulted,
Drumming, feasting and rejoicing were grand;
For the GODS he confirmed, had consented,
To allow them work freely on the land.

The farming season was the crucial test,
Crops grew fast and harvest a great success;
All agreed that JUJUMAN was the best,
As he invoked to save them from distress.

But the Quack had become a virtual pest,
Whose threats and harassments were in excess;
When he sensed that he was trapped in earnest,
Soon escaped leaving many, many more to confess.

RIVER CAVALLA FLOWS FOREVER

The Cavalla flows gently to the South,
Disgorging sand and silt from its mouth;
It flows with Grace so mighty,
A might of power and quiet dignity,
River Cavalla flows forever.

It utters a fearful sound at its falls,
As nothing that drifts along ever stalls;
But creates a sense of ownership,
Among canoe owners who dwell in fellowship,
River Cavalla flows forever.

It is a source of endless livelihood,
For farmers plowing its banks in brotherhood;
In spite of constant disappearances,
These disappearances not covered by insurances,
River Cavalla flows forever.

River Cavalla is no respecter of persons,
As it overpowers various groups and ranks by dozens;
The high tides shield her inner will,
A will that lures many wailers down the hill,
River Cavalla flows forever.

ALOYSIUS K. ITOKA

River Cavalla does not sleep at night,
It's strong undercurrent is never in sight;
So many often fall into this unseen nest,
That nest sends them forever to rest,
River Cavalla flows forever.

A story is often told of two teenage girls,
Who underestimated the cunning swirls;
The sun had presaged a bright and lovely day,
A day that would have led them astray,
River Cavalla flows forever.

Into the dark muddy waters they quickly plunged,
Encouraged by a frail looking lad slightly hunched;
Below they went immersed in a body of such great size,
A size with which onlookers could do nothing but sympathize,
River Cavalla flows forever.

It is a tradition well respected by all around,
That each year so many are carelessly drowned;
In spite of this they never give up swimming,
Persistent swimming which leads to so many dying,
River Cavalla flows forever.

Nyaake once a bursting commercial center,
Then gateway to the South Eastern trade theater;
Business boomed as merchants flourished,
They flourished buying fresh vegetables to be nourished,
River Cavalla flows forever.

As River Carriers gave way to land transport,
Traders and shoppers no longer had support;
Residents in search of needs flocked to the road,
Trekking the main road each with his own load,
River Cavalla flows forever.

Rumors spread quickly that a Hydro would be built,
So those who did not wish to share the guilt;
Became indeed bewildered and confused,
So confused many hastily vamoosed,
River Cavalla flows forever.

Nyaake is now a deserted township on the Cavalla,
Which sleeps vainly to the casual traveler;
A faithful few clinging desperately for their living,
Just living which keeps the community from dying,
River Cavalla flows forever.

ALOYSIUS K. ITOKA

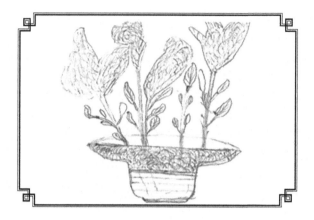

LET PEACE PREVAIL

Let Peace Prevail in the hearts of men,
Whose lives have been emaciated by hate and Savagery;
And subjected to humiliation and indignities,
In the hearts of men, Let Peace Prevail.

Let Peace Prevail in our society,
The embodiment of cultural, ethical and traditional heritage;
Where civilized elements who have lost their conscience,
May be brought back into sanity in our society, Let Peace Prevail.

Let Peace Prevail in schools throughout Liberia,
Where the future custodians of the land would be taught;
The fundamentals of citizenship and prepare themselves,
For selfless services to the State,
In schools throughout Liberia, Let Peace Prevail.

Let Peace Prevail in all Churches,
So that we shall be able to share in the work of Creation;
And be blessed to assist the Prelates and all others dedicated to
His Services,
Carry out the work of Salvation by winning more souls for Christ,
In all Churches, Let Peace Prevail.

ALOYSIUS K. ITOKA

Let Peace Prevail on the streets of Monrovia,
Where God's People will be left to walk in Freedom;
To freely socialize void of the fear of a grenade,
Where suspicion and fear will be replaced by confidence and faith,
On the streets of Monrovia, Let Peace Prevail.

Let Peace Prevail in the market place,
So that the poor and unfortunate may be allowed peace of mind;
Freedom from want, harassment and molestation,
In the market places, Let Peace Prevail.

Let Peace Prevail on Election Day,
When friends and foe alike, renouncing hostilities and hatreds;
Will accept peace and the ballots,
Thereby erect a solid National Foundation to set our Nation Free,
On Election Day, Let Peace Prevail.

Let Peace Prevail on Capitol Hill,
Where the Executive and Legislative branches remain distinct;
And the Chief Executive remain the TENANT of the PEOPLE,
PROTECTOR and DEFENDER OF THE CONSTITUTION:
On Capitol Hill, Let Peace Prevail.

Let Peace Prevail in our gracious land,
From guns of destruction and missiles unkind;
Over Nimba Heights and the Coast of Sinoe, across the country;
From the banks of the Cavalla to that of Mano,
In our Gracious Land, Let Peace Prevail.

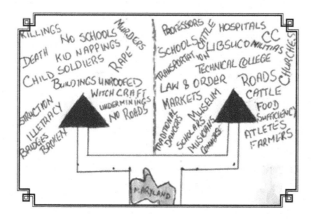

WHICH WAY MARYLAND

They came like birds on a farm at harvest,
With weapons gleaming and arms from the West;
To blow up the Churches, City and ALL,
So as was designed Maryland is saved;
Which way Maryland, which way,
Thank God, Thank God that He has spoken,
And Maryland is set Free by God and not Man.

O land of peace and happiness we know,
Where are the stalwarts once brave and so bold;
Did they not flourish throughout this dear Land,
Lawyers and Statesmen, Musicians at hand,
Churchmen and Scholars, Professors alike;
Which way Maryland, which way,
Thank God, Thank God that He has spoken,
And Maryland is set Free by God and not Man.

Are all your glories now truly ended?
And agile dancers no more fleet-footed;
Is this not the Land of milk and honey,
Where lies the symbol of greatness and fame,
Which way Maryland, which way,
Thank God, Thank God that He has spoken,
And Maryland is set Free by God and not Man.

ALOYSIUS K. ITOKA

Maryland O dear, you are of the East,
Are you now condemned to become the least;
Your Old are sick, ignored and dejected,
The Strong so bored, jobless and rejected,
Sadly surviving, obeying the breeze;
Which way Maryland, which way,
Thank God, Thank God that He has spoken,
And Maryland is set Free by God and not Man.

Out of the carnage although unbroken,
Schools are plundered many homes forsaken;
The streets are lonely your course uncharted,
Lives and values remain unprotected,
Give thanks to Him for His Presence is Great;
Which way Maryland, which way,
Thank God, Thank God that He has spoken,
And Maryland is set Free by god and not Man.

Large herds of livestock once grazed Greboland;
Their presence and grace were part of His plan;
Where are the sheep and goats of past gone years,
The eyes of cattle will shed no more tears,
Which way Maryland, which way,
Thank God, Thank God that He has spoken,
And Maryland is set Free by God and not Man.

Beneath tall palm trees the land of our birth,
Where Cane plantations were measures of wealth;
Progressive LIBSUCO, Life of the Land,
Dismantled "TC" pride of Maryland,
FATIMA AND CUTTINGTON gone for all ages,
Which way Maryland, which way,
Thank God, Thank God that He has spoken,
And Maryland is set Free by God and not Man.

* LIBSUCO—Liberia Sugar Company

** TC—William V S Tubman Technical College

*** Fatima College and Cuttington College

ALOYSIUS K. ITOKA

KEYWORDS OF
THE POEMS

The Cavalla River

Boughs
Gloom
Scene
Suds

Embarkments
Montrous
Scuttle

Fatal
Sand-bars
Slopes

Good Old Days

Blight
Dismal
Serene
Yawning

Conceit
Dreadful
Succumed

Deceit
Frail
Twain

Have no Confidence in Man

Arrogance
Domain
Melodious
Reigns

Commited
Exalted
Rebellious

Debased
Heathen
Righteous

He is Lord

Dreary

Lame

Precious

Weary

Groan

Maimed

Putrid

Horrors

Marshes

Revenge

I Heard No Rooster Crow

Bleak

Emitting

Stench

Vain

Decade

Marvelled

Trailing

Deployed

Remorse

Unending

The Dissappointed Policemen

Bemused

Congenial

Scarlet

Trailing

Clan

Culprit

Shear

Clod

Dismay

Tread

Live not in Disgrace

Arrayed	Azure	Bedecked
Blurred	Charming	drenched
Faint	Gait	Plight
Reflect		

Lizards, Lizards Everywhere

Casually	Cringing	Dangling
Despondents	Inmates	Nightmares
Roam	Reptile	Sneak
Wink		

The Juju man

Creeks	Crucial	Crusted
Disarray	Discontent	Fetters
Gibbons	Gloomy	Havoc
Invoked	Misfortune	Omen
Oracles	Quack	Reserve
Snare	Vengence	Virtual
Wrath		

River Cavalla Flows Forever

Bewildered
Deserted
Immersed
Presaged
Silt
Trekking

Boomed
Disgorging
Lures
Respecter
Stall
Utter

Bursting
Frail
Persistent
Shield
Swirls
Wailers

Let Peace Prevail

Citizenship
Emaciated
Heritage
Suspetion

Creation
Embodiment
Humiliation
Tenant

Dejected
Ethical
Sanity
Void

Which way Maryland

Agile
Designed
Gleaming
Plundered

Carnage
Fleet Flooted
harvest
Stalwards

Dejected
Flourished
Measures
Symbol

Printed in the United States
By Bookmasters